WHO ARE

LANDY VICTOR

Dedicated to my LORD JESUS CHRIST, my Saviour. Thank You God the Father and Jesus Christ the Son for inspiring me (through the Holy Spirit) to write this book.

Contents of the book

1. **About the author**
2. **Introduction**
3. **Who are you?**
4. **Tips on how to build up the Spirit of God in you**

1. **<u>About the author</u>**

My name is Landy. I am a graduate in Law and mother of two. I attend church services at **New Life Revival Church (NLRC)** in the Merseyside.

I have lived my life to be a God Warrior. I happened to have the love of God since I was a little girl. The devil saw this light in me and tried to destroy it, so that God would not achieve His purpose in me. But he failed because God who lives in me is stronger and greater than that who is in the world. Today, I am here doing the WILL of God in my life.

This book is useful to Christians and non-Christians.

2. **<u>Introduction</u>**

WHO ARE YOU? Which side of this world do you belong to? The Good Side? Or the Bad Side? According to me, there are two categories of people in this world: the Good Side and the Bad Side. And these categories of people can be found within all the different continents of the world. If you are reading this book, that means you are interested in finding out who you are. I don't know about you. But as for me, I am a child of God. I am a God Warrior. I don't play the devil's tricks – I fight the enemy. I have never lost a battle with the enemy before, though it's difficult when fighting those demons. But in the end I always get them stranded, disarmed.

Genuine children of God across the world, all together, we form an Army of Good Angels on earth. I call us **Angels of the Good Side**. We are the body of the church and the church belongs to Christ Jesus. Our mission is to continue passing the **message** of our Lord Jesus Christ on to the entire world for it to be saved. This message is the message of **salvation**. It does not matter what you are doing now or what you have done in the past. What matters now is that you repent from all your wrongdoing and accept that Jesus is Lord and Saviour. Salvation is not about you doing wrong. It's about the fact that Adam and Eve sinned, and that through them we all became sinners and needed to be saved from our sins.

The Bible (in Genesis, chapter 3) tells us that as soon as Adam and Eve had eaten the fruit, they realised that they were naked. But they were naked before, they just didn't know it until they had sinned. And we could argue that Adam and Eve must have noticed a change in their bodies, when really there was no change in their bodies but rather in their mental state. They became aware of something. And this awareness was the knowledge of sin. This book will help you be aware of your sins (the bad things you do in your life). It will help you examine your mind by distinguishing good thoughts from bad thoughts; because the way you think is the way you will act. The book will help you make a change in your life by eliminating all the bad things about you, turning yourself into a good person/angel.

And after they had sinned, God said to the woman that He would increase her trouble in pregnancy and her pain in giving birth. And because the man had listened to his wife when seduced to eat the fruit, God said to the man that the ground would be under a curse. He would have to work hard and sweat to make the soil produce anything, until he went back to the soil from which he was created. We as humans became mortal.

Angels of the Bad Side – not only does the Bible talk about them out loud and often refer to them as demons or the devil, if you like, but also I am now telling you myself that they are not good at all. They cause a lot of damage to the world. I have met several of them. They all have the same symptoms: They wink. They argue. They are jealous. They steal. They invent lies. They kill. They cause war. They hate. They covet. They mock. They gossip. They insult. They negatively envy. They are arrogant. They doubt. They compete. They cause strife. They lust. They scoff. They deceive. They rebel. They cheat. They are conceited. They boast. They have a bad temper. They are unholy. They are selfish. They have a party spirit, etc.

Bad angels do so many bad things that the list is endless. They are inspired by the devil. Mark my words that you wouldn't want to be an angel of the Bad Side. Their reward is as bad as hell. I am not being cheesy, but it is a reality you will come to discover as you read this book.

3. <u>Who are you?</u>

Today, my message to you is: WHO ARE YOU?
According to the Bible, we have a creator who created
us through His image. **Genesis 1:26: Then God said,
"And now we will make human beings, they will be
like us and resemble us. They will have power over
the fish, the birds, and all animals, domestic and
wild, large and small" (Good News Bible, 1992).**
And indeed this is a fact. The world is inhabited by
men and animals, though some scientists might state
otherwise.

The 'who you are' determines your character: the way
you live your life, the way you talk and behave, the
way you listen to yourself and to others, the people you
stay around with, the way you react to situations, the
way you reflect back to others, **but most importantly,
the way you think.** Your actions are the fruits of your
thoughts. Your thoughts are like seeds. When you
think of something, whether it is a good thing or a bad
thing, it is like you are sowing a seed in your mind of
'that something' which will later become a concrete
action. I hope this book helps you improve or change
the 'who you are'.

So, Man who are you? According to the Bible, you are
a creature of God. And that God gave you power! So

you have **power** within you! And what is this power? You will come to know what this power is by the time we get to the centre of the message. But only bear in mind that this power is 'the power to do good' and not to do evil.

The Bible goes further to tell us that God then made a woman as a suitable companion to help man, as none of the animals were a suitable companion for him. God made the man fall into a deep sleep, and while he was sleeping, God took out one of his ribs and closed up the flesh. God formed a woman out of that rib. That is why a man leaves his father and mother and is united with his wife, and they become one.

So, Woman, who are you? Just like man, you are a creature of God. You have the same **power** as man. Today, I want you to ask yourself, who are you? Take a God look at yourself right now, and answer this simple question.

1. Who are you? (Are you a child of God?). I give you a few seconds to answer this question.

Have you answered the question? If you are a child of God, then this message is vital to you, in order to evaluate yourself and see if you are really what you claim you are. And if you are not a child of God, I still want you to carry on reading, and then decide for yourself on which side you want to belong: God's side, which is the Good Side, or the other side, which is the devil's side.

Now, remember what we said at the beginning: that God made you to be like Him. Now who is God? **John 1:1–5**, says: **In the beginning was the WORD, and the Word was with God, and the Word was God. He was with God in the beginning. Through him all things were made; without him nothing was made that has been made. In him was life, and that life was the light of all mankind. The light shines in the darkness, and the darkness has not overcome it (Holy Bible, New International Version, 2011).**

So God is the WORD. The Bible is the word of God. 2 Timothy 3:16–17 confirms this by saying that all scripture is God-breathed and is useful for teaching, rebuking, correcting and training in righteousness, so that the servant of God may be thoroughly equipped for every good work.

And God spoke the WORD out of LOVE. He did everything for love. **1 John 4:7–10** confirms this: **Dear friends, let us love one another, for love comes from God. Everyone who loves has been born of God and knows God. Whoever does not love does not know God, because God is love. This is how God showed his love among us: he sent his one and only Son into the world that we might live through him. This is love: not that we loved God, but that he loved us**

and sent his Son as an atoning sacrifice for our sins (Holy Bible, New International Version, 2011).

And when God spoke the WORD, the word came into ACTION. So our God is a practical God. He said, let us make man, and man He made. So we are supposed to be practical Christians. James 1:22–23 clarifies that we should not merely listen to the word and so deceive ourselves. We need to do what the word of God says. Anyone who listens to the word but does not do what it says is like someone who looks at his face in a mirror, and, after looking at himself, goes away and immediately forgets what he looks like. So for example, let's say you wake up one morning, ready to go to work. You look at yourself in the mirror and find that you have discharge in both your eyes, but immediately, without washing your face, you put on your uniform and you go straight to work. Why haven't you washed your face? What will people think of you? The effects of practising the word of God turn out to be like a reflection in a mirror, where you can look at yourself and often analyse how well you are doing in terms of being a practical Christian. This mirror is very significant, because it reflects every act you do; this mirror turns out to be your personal record of your life. From this comes improvements which make you a better person.

Now, you who claim to be a child of God, do you have the following three fundamental elements of God, or in

other words, do you have the Spirit of God? They are:
1. The word of God,
2. The love of God and
3. The practice of the word of God.
I give you a few seconds to think about this.

You, who claim to have the Spirit of God and yet live in the darkness – you do not have the Spirit of God, because God is light. 1 John 1:5–7 clearly explains that God is light and in Him there is no darkness at all! So if we claim to have fellowship with God and yet walk in the darkness, we lie and do not live out the truth. But if we walk in the light as He is in the light, we have fellowship with one another, and the blood of Jesus, His Son, purifies us from all sin.
One day, I guess it was in 2009, I watched a video of a young lady who claimed to have known Christ but was still committing so many immoralities. She would get drunk, she would flirt around with men, and she would do all these bad things. Later she decided to convert to some religion because she had agreed with herself that Christianity was not right. And the first reaction I had was I laughed. Seriously, I laughed. You know why I laughed? Because she lied. She never had the Spirit of God and had never known Christ. Because the Scripture says, 'If you have the Spirit of God and yet live in the darkness you lie', because God is light. How

can you say you know Christ and do all these bad things?

Now, if you are not manifesting the Spirit of God yet, that means you are still a sinner. You are still in the world of darkness. But the good news is you can still be born again. I will explain to you why you are not saved yet.

Because Adam and Eve sinned when they ate the forbidden fruit, at that same time we all sinned. We came to know what evil is and how to do evil, and automatically we lost the Spirit of God. We got ourselves separated from God. Why did we all sin when physically we were not there when this happened? Like I said before – the sin was not physical sin; it was *mental* sin. And according to the Bible, Adam and Eve were the first people God created, and all human beings descended from them. So the mental sin transferred from one descendant to another. Then God brought the law through Moses to make us clean again. But again, we failed to meet the demands of the law. Why? Because we brought evil into the law. Instead of dealing with the law in God's way, we dealt with the law according to the flesh, according to our desires. So the law become unbalanced. And that is why today the world is not equal. Some people are happy and others are suffering. To live according to the flesh is a sin to a child of God because the flesh does not know the Spirit of God which our spirits are appealed to know. The flesh is weak and on its own cannot satisfy God. The Bible tells us that what the law was powerless to do for us because it was weakened by the flesh, God did by sending His one and only Son in the likeness of sinful flesh to be a sin offering. By doing this, God condemned sin in the flesh in order that the righteous demands of the law which we failed to meet (because we brought evil into the law) might be fully satisfied in us who do not live according to the flesh, but according to the Spirit of God. So people who live according to the Spirit of God are no longer under the condemnation of the law but under the grace of Jesus. But people who live according to the flesh aren't, because they have their minds set on what the flesh desires, so they will be judged for their sins; therefore they are under the condemnation of the law (that is death).

People who live in accordance with the Spirit of God have their mind set on what God desires, and the mind controlled by God is life and peace. If you have a Bible, you could later read Romans 8:3–7 for more clarification.

Until Jesus, Son of God, came to save us from sin and the unfairness of the law, we were not saved!

My question to you now is this: Who are you? Are you the type of person who lives his or her life according to the flesh rather than in accordance with the Spirit of

God? Are you still a sinner? And if your answer is *yes* to either of the last two questions, then I say to you – it is time for you to be born again!

To be born again is also called salvation (being saved from sin). According to my own experience of salvation, it could be said to consist of a four-step procedure: repenting, confessing, believing and receiving. Why four steps? Because they work along together in order for salvation to be a success. For example, after you have repented, you will have to confess; after confession, you will have to believe in Jesus Christ, and once you have believed, you will receive the Spirit of God.

A. REPENTANCE

Biblical repentance means to change your mind in regard to Jesus Christ. It's like being given a new mind by God to replace your old mind. Your old mind is gone. **Romans 12:2** says 'do not conform to the pattern of this world, but be transformed by the renewing of your mind. Then you will be able to test and approve what God's will is – his good, pleasing and perfect will'. When you make a decision to repent, you make a decision to come out of the darkness and to go straight into the light. Know that you make a significant transfer, and you could call this transfer 'the beginning of salvation' that is, to 'be born again'. At this stage your mind is made up to follow Christ Jesus, and the next step is to confess, believe and be baptised. But when you decide not to repent, you decide to remain sinful all your life, because life in the darkness is all about evil, poverty, drugs, sexual immorality, disrespect, arrogance, pain – you keep on hurting people. If you are a wife, you keep on hurting your husband. If you are a husband, you keep on hurting your wife. If you are a parent, you keep on hurting your children, and if you are child you keep on hurting your parents. That is how it is to live in the darkness. You are blind; you don't live righteously. That is why the devil loves the darkness, because that is where he keeps people enslaved to sin. The devil has no compassion at all.

After you have repented, you will notice a huge difference in your lifestyle. Your mind will change its ways of thinking, acting and of giving and receiving information. You will no longer think and act the way you used to. The old you will be gone. It will be the new you. You will start to think and act as Jesus Christ. You will no longer be blind. The light of God will have opened your eyes.

I will briefly explain what it is to repent. I see repentance as the first change to the old mind because repentance is just the first stage of salvation or the beginning of salvation, if you like. In **Matthew 4:17**, when Jesus began to preach, He said, "'Repent, for the kingdom of heaven has come near'". So the first thing you have to do in order to start a relationship with God is to repent. John the Baptist used the same words as Jesus, when he was preaching in the wilderness of Judea (**Matthew 2:32**). In **Luke 5:32**, Jesus responded to the Pharisees: "'I have not come to call the righteous, but the sinners to repentance'". In the Oxford Dictionary of English, to repent means to feel or express sincere regret or remorse about one's wrongdoing or sin. In my opinion the Oxford definition does not detail the renewing of mind, in the sense that you can regret an act of wrongdoing, but you fail to change your mind to avoid the same mistakes from happening. But Biblical repentance means to 'change one's mind'. **Ephesians 4:23** says that Your hearts and minds must be made completely new. By changing your heart, you are also changing your mind. So it is an intentional change of mind and an act of turning away from sin. There must be what I call '**intent to repent**'. You must show God that you have an intention to repent. Then **you prove that intention through an act**. If you have no intention to repent, though you could still get baptised, you will never grow as a normal Christian should because you are double-minded (half in the light and half in the darkness). Therefore do not repent because you feel like you need God. That feeling could fade away. Repent because that is the right thing to do. In **Isaiah 1:16–17**, God says: 'Wash and make yourself clean, take your evil deeds out of my sight. Stop doing wrong, learn to do right'... This makes it clear that to repent is the right thing to do.

As you carry on reading this book, I expect you to develop 'an intention of becoming a child of God, following this with the act'. So for example: you regret living in the darkness; you decide to come out of it. You put an end between you and the devil because you are not going back in the darkness. You look for a good local church, you start attending church services, and then there, you confess your sins and get baptised. So by then you must have believed that Jesus is LORD AND SAVIOUR.

If you are already born again but still live in the darkness, that means from the time you were baptised until now you failed to renew your mind. This means you temporarily renewed your mind, and you are in breach of covenant with God. What you need to do is confess your sins again and renew your covenant with God. Bear in mind that when you repent, the 'renewing of mind' or the 'change of mind' is permanent or infinite and not temporary.

Many people repent without having an intent to repent. And what often happens is that, because they have no intention to repent, they temporarily renew their mind and then tend to go back to their old lifestyles. Those types of people hardly progress in their Christian life because they are not serious about the word of God. They do not have the word of God as their foundation. They are neither cold nor hot.

There are many reasons why people fail to show a genuine intention towards repentance. We have those who temporarily repent because they are looking for something such as comfort, empathy, healing, or financial help, or there may be some other reason behind their conversion in Christ. Upon their conversion in Christ they look forward to receiving their needs from God. They know what God is capable of. And when they become impatient in waiting, they stop going to church; they give up on God and the devil comes back into their lives and replaces the old mind.

We also have those who do receive what they have asked for, and after they have received it all, they feel they don't need God anymore. They go back to their old lifestyles.

B. **CONFESSION**

After you have repented, you will have to confess your sins. So as you turn your face towards God, you are saying: "Father Lord, here I am. I have sinned against you and I want to confess my sins." In real life, this is done in your chosen church with your pastor or the church leaders. So what is confession? Biblical confession is a genuine declaration of your sins. You admit your sins and accept to be saved by our Lord Jesus. **1 John 1:9** says 'If we confess our sins, He is faithful and just and will forgive our sins and purify us from all unrighteousness'.

Romans 10:9–10 emphasises that 'If you declare with your mouth "Jesus is Lord", and believe in your heart that God raised him from the dead, you will be saved. For it is with your heart that you believe and are justified, and it is with your mouth that you profess your faith and are saved'. Therefore this declaration is very important because it is what determines your 'intent to repent'. Do not joke about it. Do not confess when you know in your heart you have not really repented. You will be making a fool of yourself. And if you do confess without a genuine intention, you will never grow as a normal Christian should because you are half in the light and half in the darkness. And with God you cannot have your other half in the darkness; you either confess your sins again, this time with a genuine intention of bringing that half of you which is in the darkness into the light, or you are not a child of God. **Romans 8:16** says 'The Spirit of God himself testifies with our spirit that we are God's children'. So if you are born again but still live in the darkness, you are not a child of God.

A genuine child of God respects his or her new mind, protecting it from sin. He or she, on a daily basis, feeds on the word of God in order to face the difficulties and challenges of life.

I ask you today: are you ready to confess your sins? To those of you who are born again but live in the darkness, I ask: are you ready to confess a second time?

Do not be ashamed to confess your sins. We have all sinned in one way or the other. We all became sinners when Adam and Eve ate the forbidden fruit. **Romans 3:23** says 'For all have sinned and all fall short of the glory of God'. So do not conceal your sins. Set yourself free today. **Proverbs 28:13** tells us that 'whoever conceals their sins does not prosper, but the one who confesses and renounces them finds mercy'. **Romans 5:8** clarifies that Jesus died for us 'while we were still sinners'. So open up and be genuine. You are not going to tell the church what wrongs you have done. It is a declaration given to you by the church itself which you repeat after the pastor or the church leaders. It shall be well with you. In **Isaiah 1:18** God is telling you: "'Come now, let us settle the matter … Though your sins are like scarlet, they shall be as white as snow'". So come forward, okay?

C. BELIEF

As you read the section on confession, you came across **Romans 10:9–10** from which I am going to extract specific words relevant to **belief**, words such as 'and you believe in your heart that God raised him from the dead, you will be saved. For it is with your heart that you believe and are justified'.

Just like repentance and confession, **belief** requires that you have an '**intent to believe**' in Jesus Christ. God knows if you believe in Him or not, and I would want to emphasise that your intention in becoming a new creature in Christ must be established from the very first stage of salvation, which is repentance. You must have already shown this intention when you repented. It is this same intention that helps you confess, believe and receive. It's like a formula: Intent to Repent + Intent to Confess + Intent to Believe + Intent to Receive = SALVATION.

Now, how do you believe in Jesus? You do not only declare with your mouth that Jesus is Lord; you must thoroughly believe that that is what He is, taking into account what the Bible says about Jesus. So, firstly, you believe in Jesus by believing in the WORD of God. That what the word of God says is TRUE! That that word has an impact on you. It was written for you to read and retain. The word of God is like a property you keep hold of. In **John 5:24**, we have Jesus saying "'Very truly I tell you that whoever hears my word and believes Him who sent me has eternal life and will not be judged but has crossed over from death to life'". And why must you believe in the word of God? Because God Himself is the WORD. **John 1:1** clearly tell us that: 'In the beginning was the Word, and the Word was with God, and the Word was God'. And **Genesis 1:3** says: 'And God said, "Let there be light", and there was light'. So God used words to create heaven and earth, including human beings. God put words into His Son for Him to speak out on His behalf, just as He had put words into Noah, Abraham, Moses and all the rest of the prophets. And where do you find the word of God? In your Bible. So bring out your Bible today! Now many of you could be thinking, "why are we saved by Jesus but must believe in the word of God?" Well, I tell you, Jesus and God the Father are the same. The word of God is the same as the word of Jesus. The Bible specifies that God is light, as it does of Jesus. In **John 14:6**, Jesus responded to Thomas that "'I am the way, the truth and the life. No one comes to the father except through me'". Praise God!

Secondly, you believe in Jesus by putting the word of God into practice. So **firstly** you **believe** in the word of God, and **secondly** you put the **word into practice**. In **Matthew 7:24–25** Jesus says: "'Therefore everyone who hears these words of mine and puts them into practice is like a wise man who built his house on a rock. The rain came down, the streams rose, and the winds blew and beat against that house; yet it did not fall, because it had its foundation on the rock'". In our own lives we experience difficulties, but if we are good at putting the word of God into practice, we cannot fall down. Read **James 1:22**.

I want you to bring out your Bible from whatever hidden place you have kept it and start reading the word of God. Believe in it and put it into practice, and you will see that God is going to start working in your life. Start reading all the chapters and verses in this book which are highlighted in bold. If you don't have a Bible, I suggest you order one online.

I am going to tell you a story which I strongly believe God wants me to share with you. God once gave me a vision, and in that vision there was a father standing with a small gift in his hands. His son was far away from him as he was going to his uncle. The previous day, his uncle had shown him the things he was going to give him: a car, a house, some money and a holiday. The son was happy that his uncle had shown him all these things, so on that day he was going to collect them from him. His own father, standing with the gift in his hands, was calling him back, saying "Come back to me, my son; here is my gift for you. It may seem small but it contains everything you need. All you want and need is in this small gift."

Now you can imagine this gift as small as a lunch box with a sign of the cross on top of it. But there were many little stones inside.

The father insisted, "Come, my son. Come and get your gift. It has everything you need."

The son responded, "Father, listen! You got to be kidding me! There is no way that small gift of yours has everything I need! You mean it has my car, my house and money? No way! Are you trying to convince me that that gift has all which my uncle has already given me? No way! That gift is too small to contain all of that. I need a car and a house, so I am going to my uncle."

The father insisted again, "Come, my son. Come and collect it; it has all you need."

"How come?" said the son. "It is impossible! You are lying to me, Father."

The father said, "My name is 'possible'. Come and open it, and you will see for yourself."

The son responded, "No, Father. I don't believe you."

The father was shocked and said, "My son, you have no faith in me. You do not believe in me. Faith is hope in what you have not seen yet."

Then the son left without saying a word. So what the father did was give the gift to someone else. And when that person opened it, the stones grew and grew into a big house, and inside that house was everything he needed. Meanwhile, his son went to his uncle and took the car and house off him. But the son found out that the car was damaged and that he had to pay money to his uncle if he wanted to live in the house.

This message is to tell you that God has all you need. He has got a package for you. Don't go anywhere else, but draw nearer to Him and collect your gift from Him. Keep your faith high. Keep on believing in the word of God. If you ever decided to leave God, you would lose everything God has in store for you. Do not compare yourself to others and become greedy in wanting all they have or the luxurious life they live. Have patience. Your own time will come. You don't know how other people get their money or whether they have good management of their finances. So please, do **believe** in the **word of God**.

D. **RECEIVE**

Some Christians want to receive from God without having followed the compulsory **procedure of salvation**. What they tend to do is skip repentance, skip confession, skip belief and jump straight to receiving. To receive from God is to first receive the Holy Spirit, and to receive the Holy Spirit is part of **salvation** and is called **baptism**. Some believe that they can serve God without thorough completion of each of the stages of salvation.

When you get baptised, you are dipped into water and come out again. You can see baptism as a *confirmation of your faith.* That, yes, you have repented, confessed and you believe in Christ and are ready to be dipped into water and come out, for the old you to go and the new you to emerge (**Matthew 3:11**).

Jesus himself was baptised so He could show us an example (**Matthew 3:16–17**). By being dipped into water, you come out clothed with the supernatural power of the Holy Spirit to walk the Spirit-filled Christian life. Baptism helps you acquire what I call **'The Holy Spirit Certificate'**. It is like being **stamped** by God with a **cachet**. It is this certificate that gives you access to be completely transformed into the new creature in Christ Jesus and be enabled to do His works (**Mark 16:16–18**). This is why you will see that those

Christians who don't have the word of God as their foundation but do agree to get baptised are not allowed to do the works of God, because they miss out on one or more of the stages of salvation. They fail to gain the essential knowledge of the word of God required. Until they fill in their gaps, they will remain like this. In addition to this, we have those who do try to gain knowledge of the word of God but misinterpret it, resulting in blasphemy against the Christian faith. They see themselves as servants of Christ when in reality they are not.

What you need to remember here is that, before you get baptised, you first must undergo a foundation course on salvation to prove that you have understood what salvation is all about and that you have genuinely repented and confessed, and you believe in the word of God. Secondly, between the start date of your course and your baptism, you must show God on a daily basis that you do read His word and make the practice of it essential. Then on your baptism day, as you go deep into the water, you will be confirming to God that it is indeed your intention to become His child. You will carry on reading His word and putting it into practice. And as you come out of the water, you are as new as a newborn baby (**John 1:12–13**; **3:3–21**); (**Romans 3:19–31**; **8:1–17**); (**Galatians 2:20**; **4:6**); (**1 Peter 1:23**).

Jesus did not only bring forgiveness and salvation; He also brought with Him equity above all. He built back that bridge that was broken between us and God. It is evident that God wanted to make everything new again. He wanted us to become equal, and one again, in Him. Galatians 3:28 shows us how equal we all are in Christ Jesus, and that 'there is neither Jew nor Gentile, neither slave nor free, nor is there male or female, for we are all one in Christ Jesus'.

God, clearly, revealed Himself to His Son. Matthew 3:17 confirms it again, 'A voice from heaven said, "This is my Son, whom I love; with him I am well pleased."' So when you seek Christ the Son, you also seek God the Father!

The prophets failed to completely please God because they failed to meet the demands of the law. They failed to build that bridge. David failed when he committed adultery with another man's wife. Moses failed when he killed. But Jesus never failed! Not once!

So when you live your life like Christ, you live your life like God, and at the same time you please God. Then anything you ask in His name, it shall be given to you, not forgetting that God has a time for every single thing you ask Him or for that which He intends to give you. He will not give you what you will not be able to handle because you will dispose of it.

And in the process of waiting for God's own time, this is where *belief*, *faith* and *hope* come in:

- You must believe that, 'YES, God can and will do this for me'. See **Matthew 8: 13** and **Matthew 9:27-29.**
- You must have faith in that belief. The faith to wait for God's own time. Hebrews 11:1 tells us that faith is confidence in what we hope for and assurance about what we do not see. You must have patience in waiting, knowing that God is working things out for your own good. Romans 1:17 promotes faith because it tells us that it is through faith that God puts people right with Himself. It is through faith from beginning to end. He who is put right with God through faith will live.

Now, when Jesus says in John 14:14, "'Anything you ask in my name it shall be given to you'", Jesus speaks to those who have accepted Him, believed in Him and live their lives according to His **word (John 15:5-7).** Jesus does not speak to those who live according to the flesh. Instead, Jesus talks about those identified with the three fundamental elements of God or the Spirit of God. So do not go about wondering why other Christians don't grow spiritually and don't receive from God what they ask Him. It is simply because they miss out on one or all of the elements. Some don't have the love of God. Some don't read the word of God so they wouldn't know what the principles are and how to put them into practice in their own lives. And some, they know the word, but do not put it into practice. The last element is the one which sows good seeds that produce good fruits in your life. When you **practise** the word of God, you actually sow seeds in God's heart, and those seeds will eventually grow and produce fruits in your own life. The word 'practise' is the key here, and it is often at this stage that people fail. Righteousness and blessings are acquired through the **word** of God being **effective** in your **life (New Life Revival Church).** *Therefore, people who don't receive from God are those who have not sowed anything in God's heart* **(John 15: 1-4)**. And those types of people receive their success either from doing evil or from the devil. However, there are *exceptions* to this rule. Remember we said God has His own time in giving to those He loves, so the exceptions include:

1. Those who are waiting on God's own time.

2. Those still in the *process of transformation* into the *new creature* that is when you have just been born again and need to completely **renew** your mind to that of Christ. This renewal could take time, depending upon the commitment of a person to reading and practising the word of God. After the transformation is accredited by God, then come your blessings.

3. There are those who ask for the wrong reasons. **James 4:1–3** highlights this by saying: **What causes fights and quarrels among you? Don't they come**

from your desires that battle within you? You desire but do not have, so you kill. You covet but you cannot get what you want, so you quarrel and fight. You do not have because you do not ask God. When you ask, you do not receive, because you ask with wrong motives, that you may spend what you get on your pleasures (Holy Bible, NIV, 2011).
So again, I ask you. Who are you? Are you still in the darkness and need to be born again so that you can receive your blessings from God? Are you born again but struggle to renew your mind and therefore have delayed your blessings? Do you get your blessings from doing evil? Do you ask with wrong motives? The 'how you ask' and 'why you ask for it' is crucial. If you have answered yes to any of these questions, then I advise you to carry on reading to find out what you could do to help yourself.

If you copy what other people do, you will end up at their destination. So when you are copying others, a good question to ask yourself is who are they? Are they children of God? Or, are they children of the devil? What destination are they heading to? A genuine child of God shows good examples to others.
There is no better destination than that which God has reserved for you. If you are copying the people of the world whose love is so dedicated to fashion, appearances, money, material things, etc., then you too

will end up like them. The scriptures say again in Proverbs 3:5–6 that we should trust in the Lord with all our hearts and lean not on our own understanding; in all our ways we should acknowledge Him and He will direct our paths. God's destination for you is beautiful, honourable, respectable, lovely and permanent.

I want you to be copying Christ and not the people of this world in which we live. You have a choice to make, because you have the power to make that choice. Remember I said at the beginning of this message that God gave us power, and Moses spoke about this same power in Deuteronomy 30:19–20 when he said to the people of Israel, "'I call heaven and earth to witness against you today, that I have set before you life and death, the blessing and the curse. So choose life in order that you may live, you and your descendants ...'". So you have the power to choose. And you have been advised to choose life. So use your power to make and give life, and not to destroy lives. **Romans 12:3–8** emphasises this by saying: **For by the grace given me I say to every one of you: do not think of yourself more highly than you ought, but rather think of yourself with sober judgement, in accordance with the faith God has distributed to each of you. For just as each of us has one body with many members, and these members do not all have the same function, so in Christ we, though many, form one body, and each member belongs to all the others.**

We have different gifts, according to the grace given to each of us. If your gift is prophesying, then prophesy in accordance with your faith; if it is serving, then serve; if it is teaching, then teach; if it is to encourage, then give encouragement; if it is giving, then give generously; if it is to lead, do it diligently; if it is to show mercy, do it cheerfully (Holy Bible, NIV, 2011).

I now ask you, who are you? What is your gift? Do you use your power to do good? Or you use it to do bad things?

To those of you who are genuine Christians, I thank you for being the good examples you are. And I encourage you to keep as such.

To those of you who are not born again yet – I ask you to look for a good local church to start attending church services, and tell them that you want to be born again.

To those who are born again but still live in the darkness, I want you to ask for forgiveness from God – confess again that you want to renew your mind. A Christian does not conform any longer to the pattern of this world; he should be transformed in the new life in God the Father and Christ the Son. So when you repent and accept Christ, there must be 'renewal of your mind': you no longer think or act like human beings do; your old self must be buried. You, rather, think and act like Christ. Ephesians 4:23 tells us that our hearts and minds must be made completely new.

And, to those who have been hurt by other Christians or any other person, or any other thing, and you believe that that is enough reason for you to stop serving God, I tell you – do not let temptations steal you from God. You do not stop serving God because you have experienced something bad, or because people are abusing that service of yours. When you serve a person, you actually serve God Himself. If people take you for granted, you set boundaries between you and them; this will help you continue your service in order to reach to those who sincerely need your help. God will deal with the abusers Himself, and He always has done. You just keep your faith high. Psalm 126:5–6 tells us that those who sow with tears will reap with songs of joy. Those who go out weeping, carrying seed to sow, will return with songs of joy, carrying sheaves with them.

Remember how Jesus responded to the devil when He was tempted in the desert. I want you to later read Matthew 4:1–11.

Every day, it is important for you to remind yourself of the unexpected temptations of the devil. The devil will never stop tempting you because it is through temptations that he gets people broken. So you must be ready to turn him down. But in order for you to be able to do that, you must have the word of God written in you:

- Like a helmet on your head to protect yourself from any mental/physical injuries. A mental injury not solved could later lead to a fight which could result in physical harm. You have the power to reject any negativity to your mind. Protect your mind by only letting in positive things.
- And like a belt to keep firm to your decisions.

Matthew 4:1–11 explains that Jesus was tempted by the devil after He had just finished His fasting and was hungry. The devil used this opportunity to tempt Jesus concerning food. This is to tell you and I that the devil will always wait for opportunities to tempt us, so be on your guard. And he did not only tempt our Lord once, but three times, and still Jesus stood firm and was clear about His decisions. Again, this is to tell you and I that the devil will tempt us as many times as he possibly can. We must always be spiritually equipped to turn him down every time. And how was Jesus able to do that? Jesus had the word of God written all over Him.

Many of you, and I say, many of you – you really are good people, and you love God. But there is a person or people in your lives who stop you from getting close to God. And I tell you today that I want you to let go of those people or that person! If it is a friend or friends, a boyfriend or a girlfriend, let them go! If it is a family member, try to talk sense into him/her; if they don't change, keep them in your prayers and love them at a distance, until God helps them change their ways.

God would not give you a friend or partner who would make you destroy your relationship with Him.

Do not be distracted by the devil. Do not let anyone distract you from God, such as all those pop stars and arrogant people who like to distract others with their evil riches and appearance. Run away from them. What makes a man, a man, is his inner being and not what he looks like on the outside.

God has a plan for you just as He had a plan for Abraham, but unless you let Him be in control of your mind, the devil will always stop you from having the 'true life': your true blessings.

Jesus is coming back to take that which belongs to Him. So what place have you won for yourself: Heaven, or hell?

End of message. I hope this message helps you meet up with God. Thank you. **Please read the following tips on how to build up the Spirit of God in you.**

4.Tips on how to build up the Spirit of God in you

Building the Spirit of God inside of you could also be called the transformed new life. It is no longer you who lives in your body, but it is Jesus Christ who lives in it. Your body is the temple of the Lord Jesus. Your body is where the Holy Spirit dwells and should remain (**John 14:17**).

The transformed new life starts from the time you are baptised. When I explained about baptism, I clarified that when you are dipped into water the old you is gone, and as you come out, the new you emerges. As you come out of the water, you receive the Holy Spirit or the Spirit of God inside of you, which then gives you **the power** to be transformed into the new creature in Christ. It is a transformation that has to be developed by yourself as you carry on in faith – that is, as you carry on reading and practising the word of God. The word 'transform' here means *an evidential change in the form, nature or appearance*. Therefore it means to *metamorphose*. So as you carry on reading and practising the word of God, your heart and mind, and thus your character, are enhanced, so that you become more like Jesus. Some teachers of the Bible like to use the butterfly example, where the caterpillar turns into a butterfly, but I like using the human metamorphosis, because that is what the Bible talks about (**John 1:12–13**).

Because we sinned and caused sin to remain in the world, the first birth, which is the natural birth (from a mother's womb), no longer reunites us with God: as soon as a baby sets foot on earth, he is foreseen as becoming a sinner progressively as he grows into an adult, and when he dies, he is not reunited with God. But if this baby, when mature enough to understand salvation, decides to give his life to Jesus and be born again, his sins will be forgiven, and when he dies, he is reunited with God. So through Jesus we are born again into a new person so as to be reunited with God (eternal life). The second birth is like being born a second time, but this time with a spiritual parent, which is God. There is only one spiritual parent, and that is God. This second birth is not a result of human choice to give birth to a child; therefore the birth is not the decision of biological parents but is God's decision. Just like a baby follows his or her mother's movements, so you ought to follow God's movements. You are a child of God, and God is your Father. You ought to respect your biological parents, but their decisions for your life should not prevail over God's plans/decisions for your life. For example, if your father tells you that you are not clever enough to study for a degree in medicine and that you should study business instead, and he decides to put you in a business school, that decision should not prevail over God's decision. If God is okay with you studying a business degree, then that is fine. But if God wants you to study medicine, then you must not allow your father to put you in a business school. Another example is this: if your mother is going to hell for her sins, you will not be going with her because she only gave birth to you physically and not spiritually.

Remember that the new birth is to live according to the Spirit of God and not according to the flesh. Through the Holy Spirit, Christ lives in you. Your body becomes the temple of Christ, so you must allow the Holy Spirit to dwell and remain there. The word **remain** is **key** here (**John 15:4**). What does it mean 'to remain'? It means to continue to exist or continue to be in the same state or condition. So if something is to continue, how else could we describe it? We would say it is permanent or infinite. Indeed, the Holy Spirit must permanently remain in you. And that is why *the renewing of mind* is also permanent (that is, you have to keep on reading and practising the word of God until the day God takes your breath). Therefore it becomes a responsibility to protect the Holy Spirit so that He does not flee from you. And the only thing that makes the Holy Spirit flee from you is SIN.

Now, what the Holy Spirit does when you get baptised is empower you instantly: "'... but you will receive power when the Holy Spirit comes on you'" (**Acts 1:8**). I see this power as the same power God gave Adam in the beginning, which Adam then lost when he ate the forbidden fruit. The power is then given back to us through Jesus when we are born again or baptised (**Matthew 28:18–20**). It is the power of authority and the authority to do good. So the power of authority is not for you to do evil. It is for you to do good to yourself and to others. Once you have received this power, what you then do is to let it grow by continuously reading and practising the word of God. This power enables you to do the works of God (**Mark 16:16–18**); (**Luke 10:19**).

Jesus Himself was baptised in order to show us an example. With Jesus being half human and half God Himself, this example was to prove that His human part had to be baptised because His human part was in the world, and the world is evil and under the condemnation of death. So with Him being baptised, He defeated the flesh and gave complete authority to the Spirit of God. That is why when you are born again, you defeat the flesh and give authority to the Spirit of God. You are no longer under the condemnation of death, but you have crossed from death to life. When you die, you will not suffer a second death; you will be raised to eternal life with

Christ. But those who are not born again will not see Christ – they will die a second death which will take them to hell (**John 5:24**).

Tip 1: You must love God with all your heart, soul and mind

 Matthew 22:34–39 explains that the Pharisees got together and one of them, an expert in law, tried to trap Jesus with this question: '"Teacher which is the greatest commandment in the law"? Jesus replied: "Love the Lord your God with all your heart and with all your soul and with all your mind." This is the first and greatest commandment. "The second most important commandment is to love your neighbour as you love yourself".

What the first commandment means is that you must love God unconditionally. God must come first before anybody else. You must trust God with all your heart, soul and mind. You **must have reverence for God (Proverbs 1:7).** When you love God, you become obedient to His word and it makes it easier for Him to trust you. How you prove your love for God is by being obedient towards him: you must read and practise His word with all your heart, soul and mind. So again, this comes down to your mind. What is in your mind? If you intentionally repented, you will intentionally love God. You will do anything to protect yourself from sin because it is sin that will make the Holy Spirit flee from you. And once the Holy Spirit flees from you, you become unwise and God stops connecting with you. The question to ask here is "am I capable of retaining the Holy Spirit in whatever conditions I come across?" Know that as you grow in faith, you must learn how to become capable of retaining the Holy Spirit, otherwise you will never be able to do the works of God. If you feel that you are not capable of retaining the Holy Spirit, it means you are not spending essential time with God, and the best thing to do is spend more time with Him. For example, if you usually pray three times a day, try to increase it to six times a day. If you read a chapter a day, make it two or three a day. If you hardly put the word of God into practice, try putting it into practice. If you are not keen on helping people, start being interested in helping others, because God's glory is seen through you helping others to live a better life (**Matthew 22:39**).

Now the trickiest bit here is this: why must you love God first and your neighbour second? And the answer is it is God who will show you how to love your neighbour. God tells you whether a person is good or bad and whether you should or should not connect with him or her, and He gives you the reasons why. Because we sinned and learnt how to do evil, evil has turned out to be at every corner and in every human being, unless they are genuinely born again. Therefore it is possible that when you are deciding to love someone, you could unluckily fall in love with an evil person without realising it. But when you love God first, God shows you who to approach and show your love to. Many children of God end up getting hurt in relationships/friendships because they did not put God first when deciding who they should marry or who to make friends with.

Tip 2: Love yourself as you love your neighbour

The first question to ask here is, why must you love your neighbour as you love yourself? And the answer is because you and your neighbour come from one Creator, though he or she may not be born again (read **Genesis 1:26**). So you are to see your neighbour as another human being just like yourself. How do you show that you love your neighbour? It is by showing care and attention to their needs and their problems. Our God is an empathetic God, and so you are to show empathy to your neighbour.

If you try to love your neighbour first and God second, you would be swapping **the commandments** and would become in danger of losing the Holy Spirit if the person you are trying to show love to causes you to sin. Many wicked people like to fake their appearance and character so as to win a special place in your heart. Once they have won that place, they plan how to scatter then shatter God's plans for your life. But if you love God first, before you even think of creating any relations with a person, God will help you to lift the veil off that person for you to clearly see who he or she really is on the inside, and thus you will avoid getting hurt. You can imagine this like someone is standing in front of you smiling innocently but holding a weapon to harm you. As for you, you cannot see the weapon yet because the weapon is not yet concrete for you to see it; it is in his mind where he is first planning on how to harm you. But when you put God first, what God does is help you to transpire that person's mind so to see the weapon sitting there in his mind.

In many cases, once God has shown you the right person to love, He will then Himself draw you nearer to him or her so He can use you to help that person achieve their goals for life or use that person to help you achieve your goals for life. So through you God shows His glory in another person's life or through that person God shows glory in your life. In fact, Jesus's glory is seen through us (children of God) helping others change their lives for the good, just as through Christ God made us become His *beloved children*. And this is what the glory of God is all about: God uses His children to lift up and change the lives of other people (see **John 14:12–14** and **John 15:8–12**).

What to remember here is that you should love God first and your neighbour second, and you should not love your neighbour more than you love yourself. You love your neighbour as you love yourself, so you are not to give more to your neighbour and less to yourself. You share with them by giving them whatever you can give them. You do not jeopardise yourself to give to them. When you try to put yourself at risk in helping others, you only give way to the devil to come in and use that risk by turning it into something worse and then making you believe that it's God who wanted it that way when, in fact, you made your own choice to put yourself at risk. The devil's aim is to always embrace the opportunity of risk.

Tip 3: You must understand how God works

God has so many ways of working with you, and you have to understand all those ways. And to be able to understand how He works, you need to be committed to His word. It is through reading, revising and practising His word that you become wise in understanding what He tells you or asks you to do. You need God's wisdom to guide you into making the right choices. When you make the right choices in life, you make the right decisions.

When a person does and completes what God has asked him to do, there is this obedience there which is very touching to God, and God, being a very reflective God, what He always does is to reflect back on the obedience by giving a reward **(Isaiah 1: 19-20)**.
You will not be able to sow any seeds in God's heart if you don't come to understand how He works. I ask you to read **Matthew 7:24–27 and John 15: 1-11.**
You do not meditate on and practise the word because you want to get something from God. You do it because it is your duty.
Meditation on the word is central to the life of a Christian. A Christian's mind does not stop renewing itself, because circumstances change, temptations increase and life goes on. Therefore, it is important to learn how to think and act like Christ. It helps especially in those moments of difficulty, when you find there is no way of getting out. In Matthew 4:4, *when tempted by the devil, Jesus answered,* "'Man shall not live on bread alone, but on every word that comes from the mouth of God.'"
Every time you find yourself stuck, in that nothing is going right in your life, bless God. Go back to His word. Think of those faithful moments when God has been good to you. Those testimonies should encourage you to hold onto the word of God. When you hold onto the word, it makes a complete difference compared to when you let go. The difference is that God eventually

does something about your problems. God has provided everything necessary through His word for His children to become all that He intended them to be. If we follow His plan for our lives, we can be assured of becoming that which He intends us to be.

Tip 4: Do the WILL of God in your life

You need to make God your remote control. Just as you use a remote control to direct you to a television channel you want to watch, so make God your remote control to direct you to your destination. God gave Abraham directions which led him to become a great and successful man. Let God lead you to your destination, just as He led Abraham to his destination. Abraham is one of the greatest characters in the Bible. He showed the ability to listen well to God's call. He listened to God when God called him to be His servant. God said to Abraham to leave his father's home, his country and his relatives and go to a land that He was going to show him. And that if he did that, God would give him many descendants, and they would become a great nation. God was to bless him and make his name famous, so that he could be a blessing to others. I liked it when God said to Abraham that He would bless those who bless him, but would curse those who curse him. We could argue here that, in our own lives, it may be unnecessary to curse our enemies because God will do that job for us. It is also possible to argue here that had Abraham not been obedient to God, though God had already made all these promises to him, they would not have come to pass. So obedience to God is key to a Christian's life.

Many of you know that it is not easy to leave one's own family behind and go to a land or a place where you don't know anybody, where everyone seems to be a stranger. It is not easy to change one's goals for life. Similarly, it is not easy to walk with God. But Abraham took the risk and followed God's plan for his life. Indeed, God directed him. With God there is what I call *risk-taking*. You have to take risks of losing what you have in order to gain what is best for you. I had to take so many risks in my life when God showed me the man of my life. I had to make decisions which I felt were degrading. But God gave me the *discretion* I needed. He gave me temporary freedom (to be outside of biblical rules) in order to go ahead with those decisions because that was the man He sent for me. I had to fall pregnant out of marriage to prove to the Home Office that my relationship with my fiancé was genuine, because at the time, my fiancé's immigration status was unsettled, so he could not have wedded me properly. I fell pregnant while I was still studying at university, and many students used to whisper, "How could she get pregnant when she has not finished her studies yet and is not even married?" But then, I was able to finish my studies with my pregnancy. My fiancé's immigration status improved, and he found himself a job. I became a graduate, a mother, a wife and a servant of God. God made me become all these in a short period of time. I can say that I was (and am) a happy wife. After we had settled well as a family, the question I then asked myself was this: "Would I have been happier with any other man?" My answer to this question was, no! Because out of a hundred, I chose him. But really it was God who helped me to make the right choice because He knew that I would not have been any happier with any other man but him. He was the only man I was compatible with. However, different situations would require different reasoning from God. What God did in my situation might be inappropriate in another's situation. God has His own reasons for doing things the way He sees fit.

The **will** of God is central in your life because God knows what seat is best for you to sit on. You are purified from negative choices by obeying the Spirit of God. Keep to God's commands. 1 John 5:3–4 tells us that to show love for God is to keep His commands. God's commands are not burdensome, for everyone born of God overcomes the world.
Obey the will of God in your life, and you will see the blessings that God will start showering on you.

Anything that tries to come between you and God, let it go! It is only God who has got the best life for you.

Tip 5: You must pray every day

Prayer is simply and sincerely talking to God. No special words or phrases are needed. You just speak to God in your language and in your own way (**New Life Revival Church**).

However, you could prepare what you are going to pray about so that you do not forget to mention all that you need. Although God already knows our needs, it is still essential that we mention them in our prayers. Matthew 7:7–8 tells us that if we ask, it will be given to us. If we seek, we will find. If we knock, the door will be opened to us: "'For everyone who asks receives; the one who seeks, finds; and to the one who knocks, the door will be opened.'"

Also, you could pray outside of your devotion time. You could be praying while cooking in the kitchen, while doing your shopping, etc. There are so many prayers I prayed outside of my meditation and devotion time, and God listened to them. I remember saying a prayer when I was changing my first child's dirty nappy; and I tell you that that prayer was listened to and came to pass.

It does not matter whether you pray to God the Father or Jesus the Son. It's the same thing.

Many Christians often say, "God is doing nothing for me. I pray and attend church but still it hasn't paid off." Then the questions I always ask them are these: Have you done what God asked you to do? Do you stay in line with the word of God, or are you always in and out of the word? Is your love for God only materialistic? Do you honestly love God? Because the formulae for getting results from God is as simple as this:

Meditation on the word of God + the practice of the word of God + the love of God = God's results in your life.

Anything you do without the love of God is worth nothing. 1 John 4:8 tells us that whoever does not love, does not know God.

And like I said before, God can delay your blessings unless you become mature enough in your faith and spirit.

Tip 6: Evaluate how well you are doing as a Christian

Always renew your mind to that of Christ Jesus. It is easy to start thinking unconsciously when you are hurt. It is when you are hurt that the devil starts to bring evil thoughts into your mind. So really, you must know how *to protect your **mind***.

A Christian's mind does not stop renewing itself, because circumstances change, temptations increase and life goes on. Have a devotion time where you can evaluate yourself on a weekly or daily basis to see what it is you did wrong, so you can improve on it; what it is you have not dealt with yet, so you can deal with it; who it is you have not forgiven, so you can forgive them; and what it is that is causing you to sin, so you can dispose of it.

On a day when it was raining heavily, a group of school mates were making their way to school. One of them had just bought herself some new stunning blue boots. They normally walked to school.

On that day, due to the rain, they had to cross huge muddy puddles to get to school. As soon as they approached the puddles to jump over them, that friend of theirs who had just bought new boots shouted, "No, wait! Wait!"

The others turned to her and wondered if she was okay. One of them asked her if she was okay. She responded, "I can't jump these puddles!"

"Why?" they all asked.

"Because I don't want to scratch and muddy my boots," she winked. "These are new boots. I disposed of my old ones. I am afraid I will have to take the bridge and go wait for the bus," she concluded.

So she quickly made her way to the bridge which was an alternative route to school but longer than the usual one they were all supposed to take, while the others jumped the puddles.

When they arrived at the school gate, they waited for her. She took about ten minutes longer than the normal route, which took about four or five minutes to get to school. And when they finally saw her approaching the school gate, they laughed and joked together. Smiling, she said, "Well see, I haven't got any scratches or dirt on my boots. They are as new as when they were bought. But just take a good look at yours: all muddy. They are not good to look at. You'd better go clean them off. You must have been jumping carelessly. I was very careful in walking with mine."

"Hahahaha". They all cheered.

There was a security man at the gate. He allowed the girl in the blue boots to go in for lectures, but he sent the others to first go and clean their boots because they were too muddy."

Matthew 7:13–14 says that we should go in through the narrow gate, because the gate to hell is wide and the road that leads to it is easy, and there are many who travel it. But the gate to life is narrow and the way that leads to it is hard, and there are few people who find it. When you are born again, you have to avoid every opportunity that would cause you to sin. When you are born again, you become as new as a newborn. So when you sin, it is like getting into mud which you will have to clean off again. If you don't clean off the mud (by confessing and asking for forgiveness), you will remain muddy until you do so, and this could delay you from having all that God intended to give you because you remain unclean in His sight.

While we are on earth, God gives us each an assignment to do. It is based on different criteria depending on what assignment you have been given. Individually we are to pass all the criteria in order to get our reward, so when you sin, you fail one or more of the criteria, and this delays you from progressing to your destination until you re-do and pass them. The devil uses many ways to get you into mud, but you have to avoid all those ways. The devil wants you to be going backwards. But God wants you to go forward! Now, I want you to take care of your hearts, like the young girl in the blue boots. She saw the risk of damage to her boots and she avoided it. Say this: *"I will not sin in the name of anything! But I will keep my heart clean in the name of Jesus! I will avoid any risk of sin so that I do not become unclean within!"*

Of course we could never be as perfect as God Himself. But there are serious sins which we should avoid, such as adultery, murder, kidnapping, jealousy, gossip, fighting, provocation, etc.

When you see a risk of sin coming towards you, you must avoid it. You must reject it in the Name of Jesus. For example, if someone comes to you and starts to gossip about another person, cut him or her off in a good way. Or, remain silent throughout the conversation with only your head nodding. But don't keep in your heart all that has been said. If you do keep in your heart all that has been said, the sin of gossip within the person who had come to you to gossip will not only remain in him/her but will have transferred to you who have listened. How it is done is that when you listen to gossip, it can affect the new creature of Christ Jesus in you. It can bring into your mind negative thoughts about yourself and about any other person involved in the gossip. And under biblical rules, you are not allowed to bring into your mind negative thoughts as they could persuade you to seek revenge and to hate, which results in sin. However, in some situations, it is good to remain silent rather than to cut the person off because God uses many ways to expose the enemy to our eyes. Some information is a 'must know' because we are not to be ignorant of the devil's devices. Ephesians 6:10–11 explains to us that we should be strong in the Lord and in His mighty power. We should put on the full armour of God, so that we can take our stand against the devil's schemes. Sometimes, it is never your intention to sin, but it is the way people provoke you – their way of mocking, talking or criticising you – that makes you feel you want to pay them back. But even when you want to fight back, you do not fight back physically or verbally; **you fight back spiritually**. Why spiritually?

Because if you do it verbally, the devil could twist what you say and use it against you just to cause you trouble. If you do it physically, you could bodily harm the other person, and you would be the one to lose because you could face prison. So you fight back spiritually: through prayers.

Those friends who like hurting your feelings – temporarily keep them at a distance, far away from having anything to do with you. Avoid engaging in conversations with them. If they still don't change their ways, then you permanently cut them off because you have to protect the Spirit of God in you. When they try to find you, kindly say that you are sorry, but you are very busy. By doing this, you protect yourself from harm, but also you save them from hurting you. And God who sees what you do will bless you.

Tip 7: Do not complain to God

Do not complain all the time to God about your needs. God knows that you need what you need. Philippians 4:6 makes it clear that we should not be anxious about anything, but in every situation, by prayer and petition, with thanksgiving, we need only to present our requests to God.

It is normal to feel left out regarding many things. But being in good health is the richest thing you could ever have on this earth, and money could never buy your health. Instead of complaining, give your needs or requests to God. Meanwhile, pray for those who have more difficulties than you do.

Look around you, and see how far God has taken you. Is your life the same as it was yesterday? If you were living in a block of flats, are you living in a house now? Then you will see how far God has taken you. And if, so far, so good, then your request will be: *may your will on earth be as it is in heaven!*

Jesus made it clear in Matthew 6:25 that we should not worry about life, what we will eat, drink or with what to clothe our bodies. That life is more than food, and the body more than clothes. None of us, by worrying could ever add a single hour to our lives.

And I completely agree with my Lord and Saviour (Jesus), because, personally, I have never seen where being worried has ever provided food to eat or clothes to wear. Worry makes you feel sad instead. Worry could bring into your mind negative thoughts. And when you start thinking negatively, you will later act negatively. To act negatively could mean 'to sin'.

Let me tell you this story. A father had three male children. These three were born from three different mothers and had never seen each other. The first was blind, the second was deaf and the third was normal with no disability, yet he was the one who complained the most to their father. The two disabled ones never complained. They always thanked their father for caring for and loving them. They wished to be cured one day. The third one would complain as much as ten times a day about their poverty. He wanted things like quality-brand clothing, video games, holidays, etc.

Then one day, the father said to him, "I will give you a dream tonight. And in that dream, if you decide you would want to exchange your life with any of those persons whom you will meet, then, afterwards, I shall give you anything you ask of me." Then night fell, and he had the dream.

When he woke up the next morning, his father asked him, "Have you had the dream?"

Tears started falling from his eyes. He fell down on his knees and said, "Yes, father, I did ... It was 9 p.m. As I threw myself into bed, I fell asleep immediately. Suddenly, in my dream, I found myself somewhere very dark with no one around, and I was scared. I looked around; no one was there and I saw only a big signpost on which were the words *Solution Road*. Before I decided to walk down the road, I looked at myself and said, 'I think it is time for me to end all the problems that have been disturbing me through my life. My misery will end today, my pains and sorrows will go away, my tears will be wiped dry and I will live happily for the rest of my life.'

"After saying this, I walked down the road. It was a long way, but I continued walking. For a very long time I walked, until I arrived at Solution Road. I could not believe the size of the crowd that I saw. What a crowd it was; I had thought I would be the only one there. I had not been expecting people at such a hidden and mysterious place. I started to ask each person what they were doing there, and they all told me that they had come for a solution to their problems. I asked the nature of their problems and each of them told me. I felt ashamed of myself because their problems were so much worse than mine. Their lives were utterly miserable. Their pains and sorrows were enormous compared with mine. Many of them were blind and deaf, and others had terminal diseases.

"I started thinking, saying to myself, 'Oh my God, I am the only one with such small problems, yet I dare to think I am the person with the worst difficulties in the world. I am much better off than any of these people.' As I was thinking, a bright light seemed to come from nowhere, while a disembodied male voice spoke from the light. The voice asked what we were all doing there. The crowd answered that they were there to solve their problems. The voice asked the crowd to explain their problems, which they did. I felt ashamed because my problems were too insignificant for the crowd and the problem-solver to hear, so I decided to make my weary way home. I left the crowd and walked the same route back, until I got home. When I woke up this morning, the first words I said were 'I thank God for my life and I refuse to exchange it with any of those people in the dream.'"

And that same morning, his father brought his other two disabled brothers for him to meet. Then, he really understood how fortunate he was.

Tip 8: Make God your every-time refuge

There is no greater wisdom compared to that of God! Did you know that you don't have to tell your problems to anybody for solutions? All you need to do is submit them to God, and He will find all the solutions. Proverbs 2:6–8 tells us that God gives wisdom; from His mouth come knowledge and understanding. He holds success in store for the upright; He is a shield to those whose way of life is blameless, for He guards the course of the just and protects the way of His faithful ones.

You don't always have to bring your issues to a man of God or anybody else. Talk to God when you are hurt. If you have to cry, cry to Him. If you have to shout, shout at Him. If you have to sing out your pains, fabricate a song for Him.

Advice from other human beings could be dangerous, because ADVICE plays a great role in your life! It can turn one bad situation into a good situation, or it can go the opposite way. Many lives have been destroyed through ADVICE. Many women and men have lost their marriages because of ADVICE. What is ADVICE? I see ADVICE as guidance or recommendations offered by one or two people to another person or people with regard to solving a particular problem. The advice can be positive or negative. ADVICE, when given, is left with the recipient to examine it, as good or bad. The question you always have to ask yourself whenever you are seeking advice or when someone is advising you is: to whom shall I go and seek for advice? Or, who is the person advising me? Is he a good person? The person from whom the advice comes is crucial. Because advice is like a pill; once you have swallowed it, it will have effects on your life. Therefore, advice from a bad-hearted person or a person who does not love you is destructive; it's full of deceit. It will make your problems worse by destroying everything around you, including yourself. Whenever a person is wrongly advising you, reject the pill in the Name of Jesus. That is why you really need no one to advise you about your problems. You just tell God about every matter. He will respond to you (through your thinking, giving you visions as to how to react).

One more thing I want to mention is that when you are distressed or stressed, taking refuge in holidays all the time will not help you become less stressed. Stress can go today and come back the day after. This is what most people like to do: they go clothes shopping and spend unnecessarily, they get drunk and they stir up trouble, just so they can escape from stress. Some go clubbing, etc. But I tell you that the devil will stress you as hard as he can because that is his only way to get you down his road. Until you have learnt that, when you are stressed, your first refuge should be the word of God and not doing the opposite, you will be turning around in a cycle which will lead your life nowhere. What will happen then on the day when you find yourself with insufficient money to chill out? Make God your sole refuge!

Tip 9: Protect your home

Your home is the temple of the Lord Jesus, so you must never let bad people into your home. If you do so, you will be opening doors to foolishness. It's like letting in snakes to come and bite you and your entire family. They will poison you so that you become like them. The Bible says in Proverbs 24:3–4 that homes are built on the foundation of wisdom and understanding. Where there is knowledge, the rooms are furnished with valuable, beautiful things. Wisdom only comes from God and you must bear this in mind. So if you let bad people into your home, you are giving them the opportunity to come in and chase your wisdom away. And when you are left with no wisdom, you are left with no Spiritual Army, and the devil easily takes you over.

The devil's army functions according to lies, deceit, dishonesty, jealousy, competition, violence, etc. If they don't make up lies, they won't function. They have to tell lies to hurt someone's feelings and get that person to lose his norms ... So never pay attention to their lies, because if you do, you will get hurt and you will lose your way to your destination. Pray to God. God will deal with them. Bad people don't fear God. Proverbs 14:2 makes it quite clear that, if you are honest, you show that you have reverence for the Lord; if you are dishonest, you show that you do not.

Make friends with people who have genuine fear for God. When a person genuinely fears God, he has total respect for what God created: a human being. Such friends add strong weapons to your Spiritual Army. They are a blessing to your home!

The other way of putting this is like this: see your home as a nation in its own right where you are the governor and you are bound not to allow any disorder within your territory. Surely, for your people's safety and your own safety, you would make sure that bad people are not allowed to enter.

Anyone who has not met the criteria of being your friend should not have fellowship with you in the first place. When you give bad people entry into your home, you allow bad fruits to be sowed in your home. Your home will fall as a result. Matthew 12:33 and 35 helps us to better understand why it's important that we make sure that the people we mix with are righteous people. This is what it says: 'Make a tree good and its fruit will be good, or make a tree bad and its fruit will be bad, for a tree is recognised by its fruit … A good man brings good things out of the good stored up in him, and an evil man brings evil things out of the evil stored up in him.'

Tip 10: Get married to a person who has reverence for God

When you intend to get married, you must get married to a good person. Because a good-hearted person will make a peaceful, joyful and successful marriage. But a bad person will make a tearful, stressful and painful marriage. But how do you find a good husband or a good wife?
In order for you to get a good husband or a good wife, you yourself must be a good person (you must be a God-fearing person), because if you yourself are not a good person, it will be you who will not treat the marriage right; it will be you who will make the marriage painful for the other person. So it has to balance on both sides. If you don't have a relationship with God yet, I advise you to look for God first. Draw

nearer to Him before you undertake any decisions because it's through your relationship with God that you will become wise in anticipating and in choosing the right husband or wife for yourself.

A person who has reverence for God is a person who has absolute respect for what God created: a human being.

A person who knows how to respect a human being is a person who eventually respects any person they meet in their life, including husband or wife, children, family relatives and friends.

Do not get married for appearances or money. You will be deceived! Do not get married because you have become desperate. Do not get married because all your mates are married. Do not get married because you are running away from a difficult world. Do not get married to a person because you have come a long way. Marriage is tough, I am telling you. There is no business harder than marriage. You could succeed in acquiring a degree at university, but you could fail at marriage.

A married couple become one in the sight of God. Genesis 2:24 tells us that a man leaves his father and mother and is united with his wife, and they become one. So anything the husband does will eventually affect the wife, and it is the same for the wife. Therefore, a married couple that work against each other will produce bad fruits in their marriage, resulting in adverse finances, unfaithfulness, disgrace, childcare breakdown and possibly separation or divorce. That is why it is very important that the both of you know Christ Jesus; this is because no one is perfect, but when you walk with Christ, your imperfections are reduced to a level which makes it impossible for you to hurt your partner or anybody else, whether it is you who are right or them. Matthew 12:25 ... 'And a town or family that divides itself into groups which fight each other will fall apart.'

Tip 11: Bring your children to God

To those of you, married or single, who have children, I advise you that you should start taking your children to church with you. It is very important for them to find out about God at an early age. They turn out to be spiritually equipped as they grow within their faith. They behave differently compared to those who don't attend church.

Tip 12: Choose your friends

When you make friends with people, watch out for the symptoms I have listed at the beginning of this book. If you cannot remember them, go back to the beginning of the book and have another look at them.

Check on how **godly** your friends are. Do they practise the word of God?

Jesus is humble. Friends who are not humble cannot fully be children of God, even when they claim that they are. Arrogance is one of the symptoms of the disease of the devil. The disease of the devil is called evil/sin.

When a friend starts manifesting any of the symptoms, know that evil has started working in them, and it is vital to keep them in your prayers, but most importantly, you must back off. Start setting boundaries between you and them to protect yourself from getting hurt because you can't tell what has started going on in their mind/heart or what evil they are thinking of.

A friend can plan his/her journey to your life pretending to love and care for you while he/she plots how to destroy you.

Be careful of those friends who always want to know everything about you – everything you do or you intend doing. There could be an evil intention behind all that because once they find out that all your projects are progressing, they could start being destructive towards you. This is because the evil intention could have been that they never wished to see you succeed, though they never said it to your face.

God hardly works when the devil is around you. There is one thing you have to understand: the devil always places his people around you to try and destroy you. Why? Because the devil knows that you are an Angel of the Good Side.

Now, how and when to notice that the devil's people are around you is very simple. You watch out for the symptoms. You will notice them in the way they conduct themselves: the words they say to you and the gestures they make.

Where the devil has placed his hands, God cannot work for you as He so desires because His works cannot get accomplished where the devil is. In other words, you are stopping God from doing something great in your life, or you are allowing misfortune to happen to you.

Put a stop to anybody or anything which causes you not to achieve the will of God in your life. If you don't, you are allowing whoever it is or whatever it is to get their way with your life. 'Allowing unhappiness' becomes a sin at the point when you know what is wrong, yet you don't want to do anything about it; you are reckless as to the risk of harm to you and to others. Therefore there is no difference between you who allow and the other who causes.

Be decisive about the many unfruitful people or situations that are in your life. Decision-making about

such people or situations is very important as it will help you save your life and move on positively. You can't keep on holding yourself back because of them. They will only end up destroying you unless they repent or change and become fruitful to you.
Don't settle for less with God. God has so many benefits in store for you. He is just waiting for you to cross that bridge so He can pour them all on you. And when that time comes, the whole world will see.

Forgive every person who has hurt you and move on with your life. Do not look back. God will take care of all the damage they have caused you. Forgiveness is from God; that is why the devil stops us from forgiving so that we can be locked in that past and then seek revenge. The best revenge is when you forgive your enemies and hand them over to God to carry out the revenge for you. God knows better how to pay off bad people.

Tip 13: Be willing to pay the price

In order for you to achieve God's plans for your life or the WILL of God in your life you must be willing to pay the PRICE:
- You must persevere God's will for life.
- You must listen attentively to God and do what He asks you to do, just as did Noah, Abraham

and our Lord Jesus. Apart from the old and new commandments (which we have in the Bible), God gives us, on a daily basis, *personal commandments* which we ought to carry out in order to achieve God's plans for our lives. *Personal commandments* or *assignments* are carried out with the application of the word of God (Bible) because the word of God is a series of precedents or case law on its own, intended to help us identity different situations and apply the right precedent or case law.

- You must always wait for God's prompting before you say or do something.
- You must understand that it is no longer you who lives but Jesus who lives in you through the Holy Spirit. **Galatians 2:20** says you have been crucified with Christ and you no longer live but Christ lives in you. The life you now live in the body, you live by faith in the son of God who loved you and gave himself for you. Therefore many things have to change. Things such as:
  - The type of places you go: you don't take the Holy Spirit to places such as clubs and unholy parties (what I mean by unholy parties are those parties where people come together for no good reason but to meet up with girls and boys. The only parties you are allowed to go to are church

parties, wedding parties, christenings, and birthday parties, except those of wicked people, etc.

- The type of music you listen to: you are only allowed to listen to gospel music. Any music other than gospel you should not listen to because your mind would capture words contrary to the word of God. As a result your mind becomes impure, and it then makes it impossible for God to connect with you.
- Choosing your friends: make friends with people who are **genuinely** born again.
- Your finances: you should lay down your money to support God's plans for your life and to support the church's activities, etc.
- Your lifestyle: you must avoid sin.

Printed in Great Britain
by Amazon.co.uk, Ltd.,
Marston Gate.